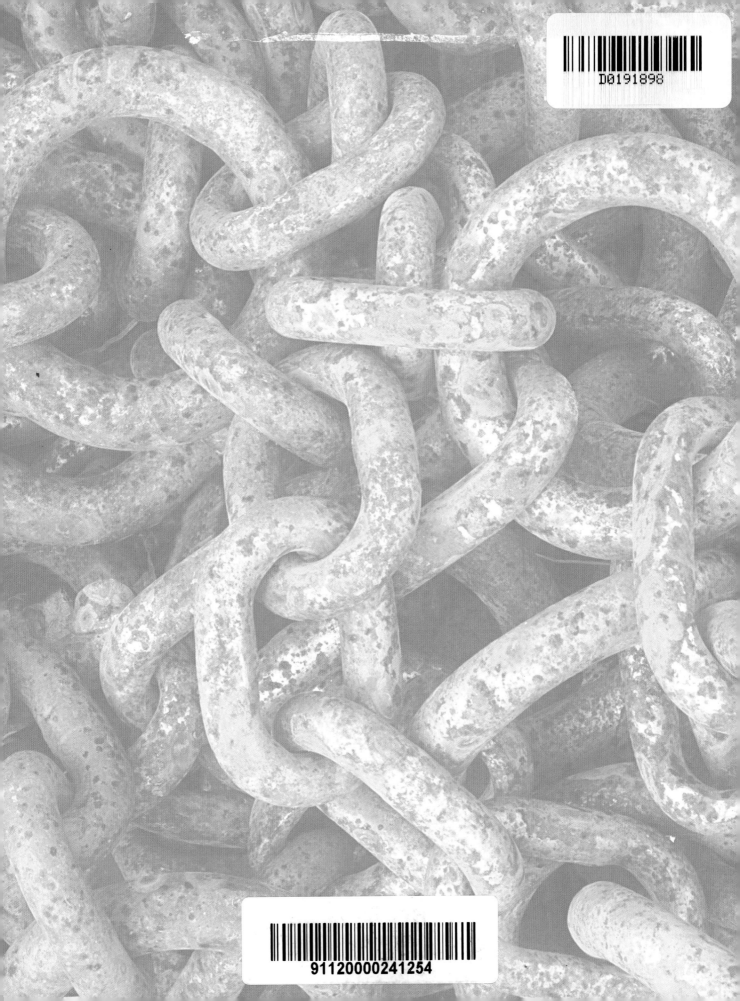

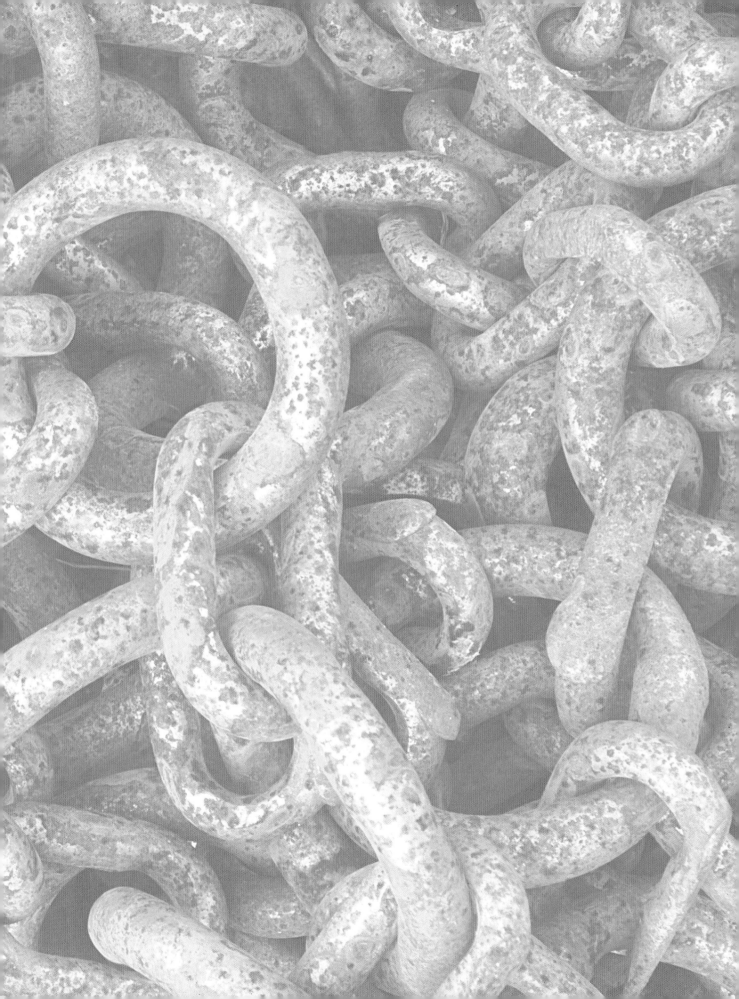

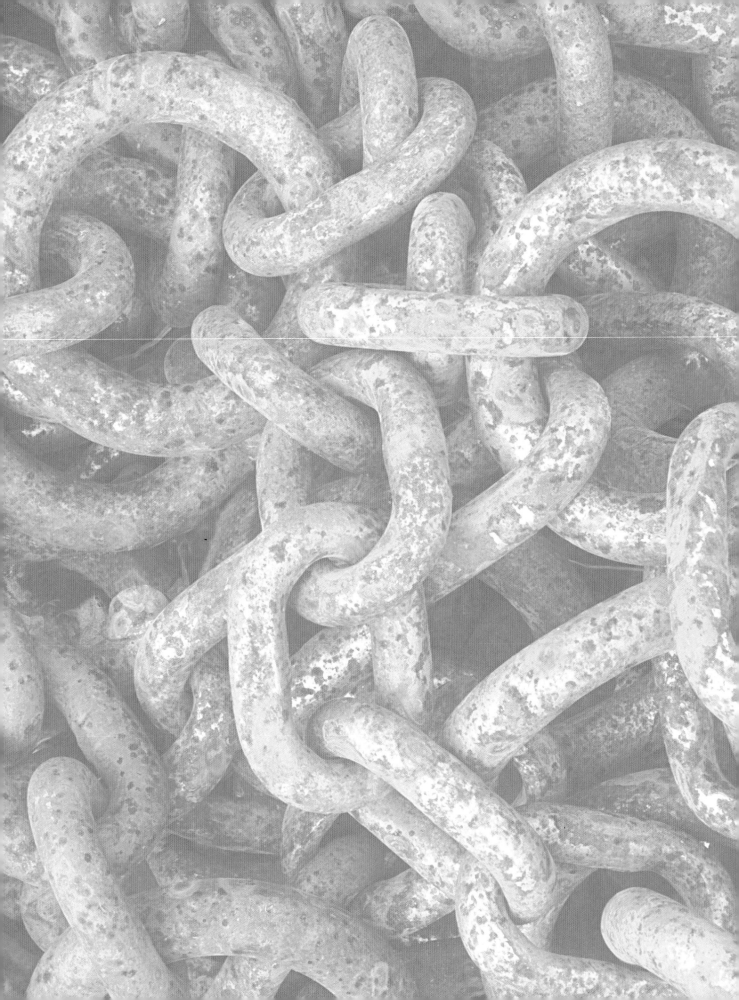

Africa and the Slave Trade

Dan Lyndon

FRANKLIN WATTS
LONDON • SYDNEY

This edition 2013

First published in 2010 by
Franklin Watts
338 Euston Road
London NW1 3BH

Franklin Watts Australia
Level 17/207 Kent Street
Sydney NSW 2000

Series editor: Adrian Cole
Art director: Jonathan Hair
Design: Stephen Prosser
Picture research: Diana Morris

Acknowledgements:
Extract from *Still I Rise* by Maya Angelou reprinted on page 9 with kind permission of Little Brown and Random House.

Abby Aldrich Rockefeller Folk Art Museum, Colonial Williamsburg, Virginia: 36. Bryan & Cherry Alexander/Alamy: 13t. Jacques Arago, Souvenirs d'un ave[...] Paris 1839-40: 31br. Art Archive: 17b. Barda Museum Tunis/G Dag[...]. Bibliothèque Nationale Paris/Bridgeman Art Library: 11b[...]UK/Bridgeman Art Library: 17t. Willem Bosman, Nauwkeurige Bes[...]ust..Utrecht 1704: 20. British Library Board, All Rights Reserved/Bridge[...]ock: 37 bg. John Elk III/Alamy: 21bl, 21tr. Mary Evans PL: 19b, 37b. W[...]/Topfoto: 5, 9t, 10tr,   19t, 23t, 26, 27b, 29b, 33b. Johnny Grieg/[...]dpapers, 4. Larisa Lofitskaya/Shutterstock: borders. [...]ulia Rome/A Dagli Orti/Art Archive: 10bl. NMM London/Picturepoint/[...]NPG/Superstock: 35b. Pictorial Press/Alamy: 39t. Print Collector/[...]. Private Collection/Marc Charmet/Art Archive: 23b. redfris[...]5b. Ann Ronan PL/HIP/Topfoto: front cover l, back cover bg, 8. Jac[...]ith/Corbis: 35t. Kyle Smith/Istockphoto: 16b. Julia Som[...]s/Istockphoto: front cover r, back cover l. Irina Tishenko/Shutterstoc[...]5 bg. Topfoto: 15tr. Sven Torfinn/Panos Pictures: 39b.

Every attempt has been made to clear copyright. Should there be any inadvertent omission please apply to the publisher for rectification.

A CIP catalogue record for this book is available from the British Library.
Dewey number: 306.3'62'096

ISBN: 978 1 4451 2323 3

Printed in China

Franklin Watts is a division of Hachette Children's Books, an Hachette UK company.
www.hachette.co.uk

Dan Lyndon would like to thank the following people for their support in writing this book; The Black and Asian Studies Association (BASA), Marika Sherwood, Arthur Torrington, Joanna Cohen and Joanna Caroussis. Thanks also to the Lyndon, Robinson, Cohen and Childs families.

This series is dedicated to the memory of Kodjo Yenga.

Contents

Introduction

Slavery has existed in parts of the world for thousands of years. As slaves, people were traded and kept as possessions to serve their owners. It wasn't until the Transatlantic Slave Trade began that so many were enslaved and transported from one continent – Africa.

Ancient slavery

There was slavery in the ancient civilisations of Egypt, Greece and Rome, and the Domesday Book records slaves living all over the British Isles in 1086. In Africa, slaves were captured as a result of wars between different tribes from as early as 3400 BCE. From the 7th century, African slaves were also traded by Muslim merchants. However, there have been no examples in history to match the scale of the Transatlantic Slave Trade that took place between the 16th and 19th centuries, at a time when trade in humans was considered by most people to be acceptable.

Transatlantic Slave Trade

The story of the Transatlantic Slave Trade is one of unbelieveable sadness; of people

▲ Enslaved Africans being brought on board a slave ship on the west coast of Africa c.1800.

of years and led to the transportation of an estimated 12–15 million Africans to the Americas. That's roughly double the entire population of the city of London today.

What's inside

This book will look at what life was like in Africa before European contact; the development of the slave trade; the journey across the Atlantic as well as life on the plantations. It also includes case studies of slaves who fought for their freedom and published their autobiographies, and it concludes by looking at the legacy of slavery for Africa. Just before you turn over, though, think about these words from world-renowned poet Maya Angelou taken from her poem, *Still I Rise*.

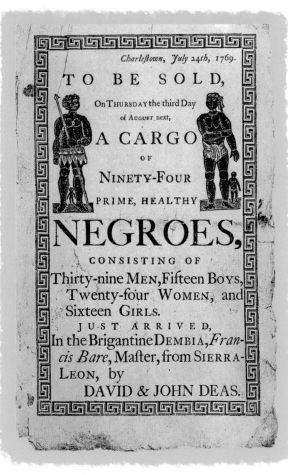

▲ *A poster from 1769 advertising 94 slaves for sale – including 16 girls.*

being kidnapped, held in prisons, shackled and sailed across the oceans in appalling conditions. But the story didn't end there. If people survived the crossing they were sold and separated from their families, and had their identity stolen from them. They were forced to work long hours under constant fear of punishment, or death, and had all of their freedom denied. And yet it is important to remember that throughout all of this, Africans resisted their enslavement at every chance. The Transatlantic Slave Trade lasted for hundreds

Out of the huts of history's shame
I rise
Up from a past that's rooted in pain
I rise
I'm a black ocean, leaping and wide,
Welling and swelling I bear in the tide.
Leaving behind nights of terror and fear
I rise
Into a daybreak that's wondrously clear
I rise
Bringing the gifts that my ancestors gave,
I am the dream and the hope of the slave.
I rise
I rise
I rise.

by Maya Angelou

Slavery around the world

The word 'slave' first appeared in the English language in the early 13th century. But slavery had existed for thousands of years beforehand, in societies all around the world. To be a slave meant you had no freedom; you had to work, usually without any payment, in harsh conditions. Forget about your own life – someone had paid for you and 'owned' you.

Slavery in the ancient world

Slaves mainly carried out jobs that others did not want to do – such as building, farming and cleaning. For example, have you ever wondered how the pyramids were built in Egypt? Some historians believe that enslaved Africans, captured in wars fought against the Egyptians, helped to build them. Slavery was an important part of the Egyptian Empire. But not all slaves were captured peoples. Some people sold themselves into slavery if they had gone into debt.

▲ *This 1400 BCE Egyptian tomb painting shows slave porters of different races carrying goods.*

There is also evidence of slavery in ancient Greece, where it has been estimated that up to one third of the population was enslaved. Many Greeks believed that certain people were 'meant' to be slaves. Slaves would do lots of different jobs including working on farms, making clothing or metalwork. Some worked as musicians and teachers. This suggests that some slaves were given enough education to be able to do important jobs.

◄ *A Greek vase from around 40 BCE. It shows that enslaved Africans were part of Greek society.*

▲ *This section of a Roman mosaic shows slaves pouring wine.*

The Romans had a saying: "*servi aut nascuntur, aut fiunt*" (slaves are either born or made). This meant that the slaves in Rome were often captured as a result of wars or were born to families already in slavery. The Romans divided their slaves into those who worked for the government and those that worked for individuals.

Slavery in Africa

Slavery existed in Africa from around 3400 BCE. But it wasn't until the spread of Islam, from around 650 CE, and the opening up of the trade routes with Muslim merchants from the Middle East in the 8th century, that large-scale trading of African slaves began. As a result, there are records of African slaves appearing as far away as the Mediterranean and into Persia. Many of these slaves were women who were used as domestic workers in the homes of their owners, but they were also sold as sex slaves. Olaudah Equiano (see pages 24–25), who was captured as a slave and taken to the Caribbean, described the differences between his experience as a slave in the West Indies and the slaves he saw as a child in Benin, Africa. Whilst the slaves in the Americas were often treated in a brutal way and had their freedom and identity stolen from them, in Olaudah's community: "*they do no more work than other members of the community ... Their food, clothing and lodging were nearly the same (as ours) ... except they were not permitted to eat with those who were born free and there was scarce any other difference between them.*"

▲ *This illustration from the 13th century shows Muslim merchants at a slave market.*

West Africa at the time of the Transatlantic Slave Trade

Some of the earliest trade contacts between European and West African people occurred from the 15th century. They came about because of the trade links across the Sahara Desert. Many African countries were rich in raw materials such as gold, copper, salt and pepper. They sold these important resources to Europeans, including the Portuguese and English.

African empires

Some empires in West Africa flourished as a result of better trade routes across the Sahara. The empires of Ghana, Mali and Songhai were all based around the huge gold fields and salt mines that were sources of great wealth. Muslim merchants travelled to the cities of Kumbi Saleh and Timbuktu to buy and sell goods, and take them to ports in North Africa, before sailing to Europe or the Middle East and India. Skilled craftworkers in Benin created 'bronzes' – many of these works capturing scenes of daily life in West Africa.

▲ A Benin bronze depicting the king's palace – notice the roof and decorative details.

When a Portuguese sailor arrived in the port of Benin in 1619, he described the city: "The streets run straight and far as the eye can see. The houses are large; especially those of the King, which are richly decorated ...The city is wealthy..."

Farming and food

Many people farmed land in West Africa, where the soil was very fertile and provided a reliable food supply of fruit, including watermelons and pineapples, vegetables, sheep, chickens and fish. However, food in West Africa changed with the influence of European traders, who bought with them spices from Asia and food from the Americas, including cassava and peanuts.

Indigo cloth

Most of the clothing worn by people in Africa at this time was made by women. They used raffia, which feels a bit like straw, and wove it into cloth. The women then coloured the cloth using a plant dye called indigo. European traders bought the indigo cloth to sell it as far away as Brazil in South America.

Music and dance

Music was also a very important part of people's lives, with many instruments being played. Drumming played a special role in African culture. It was used in different ways, including dancing, to tell stories, to send messages and for religious festivals.

▲ *Some women from Mali still wear clothes dyed in indigo today.*

▼ *Village markets in West Africa became filled with cassava (top left) from the Americas.*

The start of the Transatlantic Slave Trade

In the early 15th century, the Portuguese took over the Atlantic islands of Cape Verde, Madeira and the Canary Isles, and became the first Europeans to start trading with West Africa. In 1441, Portuguese merchants took 11 Africans to Lisbon – marking the start of the trade in enslaved Africans.

Treaty of Tordesillas

In 1493, at the Treaty of Tordesillas, an agreement was reached between the Spanish, who were 'given' most of the 'New World' of the Americas, and the Portuguese, who were 'given' Africa, India and Brazil. This opened up the possibility of connecting Europe, Africa and the Americas for the first time.

The Portuguese and the slave trade

The Portuguese were interested in developing the cultivation of sugar and realised that the conditions in the Atlantic islands, and later in South America and the Caribbean, were ideal. As a result of the expansion in the sugar industry, a workforce was needed to grow, harvest and refine the crop. The solution was to use enslaved Africans as there were not enough Europeans travelling to the Americas, and many native Americans had been killed by infection or fighting. By the turn of the 16th century, the Portuguese started to transport Africans to South America in what was to become the Transatlantic Slave Trade.

◀ *This Catalan map from 1502 shows Portuguese settlements on the west coast of Africa.*

▲ *Sir John Hawkins (1532–95) was a British merchant and shipbuilder – and a slave trader.*

◥ *The coat-of-arms of the Hawkins family – notice the bound African figure at the top.*

The British and the slave trade

It wasn't long before the British wanted to get involved in trading with West Africa. By the middle of the 16th century, British merchants were importing ivory, gold and spices from Guinea (the name given to West Africa by the Portuguese). The first record of British involvement in the trade of enslaved Africans was in 1562, when Sir John Hawkins "...got into his possession, partly by the sword, partly by other means ... 300 Negroes ... besides other merchandises." Hawkins, who was partly funded by Queen Elizabeth I, probably transported over 1,000 African slaves to the Americas.

Chattel slavery

Although there had been slavery in Africa for centuries before Europeans became involved (see page 11), there was one significant difference between the two forms of slavery. To the European slave traders, African people were seen as 'chattel' or property. This meant that they did not treat enslaved Africans as humans, but saw them as goods, like pots and pans, to be bought and sold.

Did you know?

For years, people in Europe accepted slavery as part of the society they lived in. Many believed that the lighter the skin colour you had, the more intelligent you were. Black Africans were seen as the lowest – closer to animals than humans.

The trade routes opened up by the Portuguese, and then followed by other Europeans, became known as the triangular trade because they linked Europe, Africa and the Americas together.

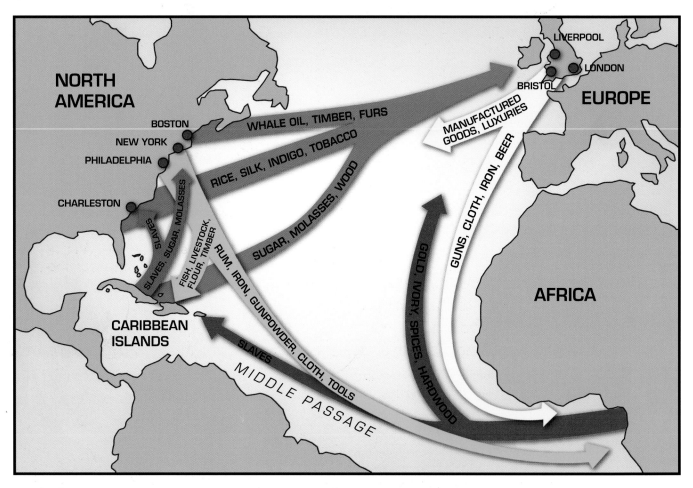

NORTH AMERICA

BOSTON
NEW YORK
PHILADELPHIA

CHARLESTON

WHALE OIL, TIMBER, FURS

RICE, SILK, INDIGO, TOBACCO

SLAVES, SUGAR, MOLASSES

FISH, LIVESTOCK, FLOUR, TIMBER

RUM, IRON, GUNPOWDER, CLOTH, TOOLS

SUGAR, MOLASSES, WOOD

CARIBBEAN ISLANDS

SLAVES

MIDDLE PASSAGE

LIVERPOOL
LONDON
BRISTOL

EUROPE

MANUFACTURED GOODS, LUXURIES

GUNS, CLOTH, IRON, BEER

GOLD, IVORY, SPICES, HARDWOOD

AFRICA

From Britain to Africa

The first stage of the British triangular trade started in the port cities of Liverpool, Bristol and London. Once the ship owners had hired a crew, which included a doctor, carpenters, sail makers and other sailors, they loaded up the ship with goods manufactured in British factories. These included guns and ammunition, pots, pans, kettles, nails and textiles, which would all be used to exchange for enslaved Africans.

▲ Map showing the triangular trade from Europe, to Africa, to the Americas and back again. The whole journey usually took a ship about a year to complete, and had to be planned very carefully to make sure that maximum profits could be made at each stage.

▲ A pistol similar to those exchanged for slaves.

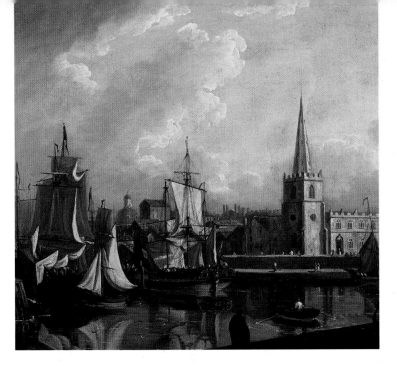

▲ *A painting showing Liverpool docks in 1797. Many slave ships left here carrying goods to exchange for slaves.*

From Africa to the Americas

The ships usually left Britain between July and September to sail to the west coast of Africa in time to avoid the rainy season. This meant that many Africans were forced to spend time in the 'barracoons' or slave prisons, whilst they waited for the slave ships to arrive. Once the British goods had been unloaded, the ships were reloaded with slaves to sail across the Atlantic on a horrific journey known as the 'Middle Passage' (see pages 22–23). They usually arrived in the Americas 6–8 weeks later. Many slaves died during the Middle Passage.

From the Americas back to Europe

As soon as the enslaved Africans were taken off the ships, they were sold off to plantation owners. The ships were then

▼ *Loading a boat with sugar barrels, Antigua, 1823. The boats were rowed out to the empty slave ships anchored in the bay.*

re-stocked with crops grown and harvested on the slave plantations. These crops included sugar, tobacco, coffee and cotton, which were taken back to Britain and sold for a huge profit.

Capture

The start of the trade in enslaved Africans in the 15th century soon grew into a huge industry, as more European countries sought workforces for their expanding interests in the Americas.

Slave industry

Slave traders from Portugal and England were joined by those from France, the Netherlands, Spain and Denmark. They sailed to the west coast of Africa and traded with coastal African tribes to provide enslaved Africans for them. Slaves were exchanged for goods, including guns and gunpowder. This meant that the African tribes who traded with Europeans became more powerful than their traditional rivals, most of whom were still fighting using bows and arrows.

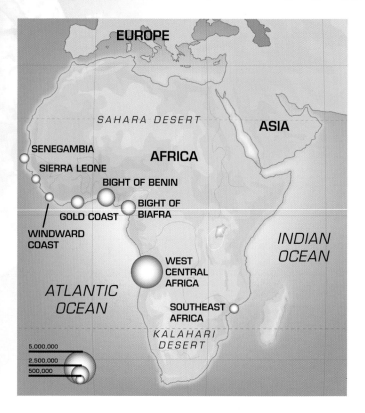

▲ A map showing the numbers of slaves exported from ports in Africa.

"One day, when all our people were gone out to their works as usual, and only I and my dear sister were left to mind the house, two men and a woman got over our walls, and in a moment seized us both; and without giving us time to cry out, or make resistance, they stopped our mouths, tied our hands and ran off with us into the nearest wood."

(Olaudah Equiano describing one method of capture – see page 24.)

Capture methods

One of the most effective ways of gathering a large number of slaves was through war. The warriors on the losing side were captured and sold. Villlages were raided, and women and children were also enslaved. In fact, a slave-ship captain wrote "*I truly believe that the far greater part of the wars in Africa would cease, if the Europeans would cease to tempt them with goods for slaves*". Another method used to kidnap Africans is described by Olaudah Equiano (left). There were also some people who had committed crimes, or broken the rules of their tribes, who also ended up in slavery.

From capture to imprisonment

Often the men, women and children who had been captured had to march many hundreds of kilometres until they reached the coastline. In fact, some of them may even have ended up working as slaves along the way before being resold into slavery. The journey to the coast was very

▲ *Slaves were bound up and marched from the African interior to the coast.*

long and many Africans died of disease and exhaustion. Once they arrived they were often put in holding pens, called barracoons, or put into slave fortresses, such as Elmina (see pages 20–21). The conditions inside were so poor that many people died.

▲ *Once at the coast, captured Africans were often held in barracoons, like this one.*

Elmina

The 'castle' at Elmina (in modern-day Ghana) was built by the Portuguese in 1482, and was the first slave trading fort in Africa used by Europeans. Captured Africans were held at Elmina while they waited to be loaded onto the slave ships.

Inside Elmina

The conditions inside Elmina were appalling, with the enslaved Africans being held in cells in the lowest parts of the castle, which had originally been used as store rooms. There were so many people crammed into the tiny spaces that there was not even enough room to lie down. Not surprisingly, diseases such as malaria and yellow fever spread easily as there was no clean water or sanitation. Then the Africans passed through the 'Door of No Return' – the name given to mark the final steps that enslaved Africans took before embarking on the slave ships to the Americas. By the 18th century, it has been estimated that 30,000 slaves passed through Elmina every year.

▲ *An illustration showing Elmina Castle, also referred to as the Castle of Saint George d'Elmina.*

This poem was written after Pelagia Nyamayaro visited Elmina in 2007 with other students from East London.

Elmina Castle

In the light mist a white-washed castle reveals itself like a ghost from the past.
Dread and curiosity leaves an unpleasant anxiety which makes you feel like a dead man walking.
Rusty old cannonballs lie on the ground, desolated like orphan children.
A painful reminder, a symbol of all humiliation and suffering one had to go through.
Mould stretches endlessly across the neglected cell walls, each bacterial pathogen lurking in the corners, waiting to ambush the weak.

▲ Elmina Castle was partly restored by the Ghanaian government in 1990, and this project continues today.

Each cell a hell of its own, damp and malodorous, the perfect torture room for terrified Africans.
Every cell bar not just a symbol of imprisonment, but a symbol of barring the captured from nurturing and developing their skills and talents.
Like imprisoned lions in a cage, every cell window facing into nowhere, a sign of freedom being a thing of the past.
In a dim-lit room you can almost hear voices, telling you the lost memories of the past.
As you walk along the pathway to the 'Door of No Return', it finally strikes you, that this was a door where only the strong and wilful walk through to live another day.

▲ These barred doorways inside are reminders of the fort's past usage.

The Middle Passage

The Middle Passage is the name given to the journey that the slave ships made across the Atlantic Ocean from the west coast of Africa to the Americas. This took between six and eight weeks depending on the weather, and ships usually left Africa towards the end of September to catch the favourable winds across the Atlantic.

Below deck

Louis Asa-Asa, a captured African, later wrote a short, shocking description of his own experiences on the slave ships:

▲ *This engraving from c.1800 shows slaves chained up below deck in crammed conditions.*

"The slaves we saw on board the ship were chained together by the legs below the deck, so close they could not move. They were flogged (whipped) very cruelly; I saw one of them flogged till he died; we could not tell what for ... The place they were confined in below deck was so hot and nasty I could not bear to be in it. A great many of the slaves were ill but they were not attended to. They used to flog me very bad on board the ship; the captain cut my head very bad one time."

Did you know?

By the beginning of the 18th century, the Portuguese had transported approximately 1 million Africans on slave ships to the Americas. However, by 1750 the British were dominant. Over the next 50 years, up to 3 million more Africans were transported. In total, between 10 and 15 million African men, women and children were forceably moved during the Transatlantic Slave Trade. This does not include those who died en route.

▲ *Slave ship plan, showing an overhead view of the upper and lower decks.*

Dreadful conditions

The space on board the ships had been calculated to fit the maximum number of slaves on board, so there was no space to stand. The slaves were forced to lie down, chained to each other. The toilets were buckets, so most of the slaves soiled themselves where they lay. If there was disease, it spread rapidly in the cramped conditions as the slaves were weak from the journey, as well as the lack of food and poor

hygiene. Alexander Falconbridge was a doctor on board slave ships from 1780–87, and he described the horrors he saw:

"The deck, that is the floor of their rooms, was so covered with the blood and mucus … that it resembled a slaughter-house. It is not in the power of the human imagination to picture a situation more dreadful or disgusting."

Above deck

At 8am and 4pm, the enslaved Africans were taken onto the deck to be fed. Their meals consisted of beans, yams and rice, and occasionally 'slabber sauce' (palm oil mixed with water, flour and pepper). They were also given water to drink. Often a man banged a drum so that everyone ate at the same time. Those who refused to eat could be whipped. Falconbridge also described sailors placing hot coals under the lips of Africans to force them to eat.

▲ *An illustration of Africans being forced to dance as part of their exercise on board a French slave ship.*

Olaudah Equiano

Olaudah Equiano was born in 1745 in Essaka, in the Kingdom of Benin (now Nigeria). He was the son of a local chief. Equiano was kidnapped, along with his sister, and eventually taken across the Atlantic where he was sold to a captain in the Royal Navy. During this time he learned to read and write, a skill which eventually allowed him to buy his freedom for £40. Equiano went on to become one of the leading figures in the campaign to abolish slavery.

The following extracts from Equiano's autobiography, published in 1789, describe some of the early experiences that he went through as a slave.

The Middle Passage

After being kidnapped, Equiano worked as a slave for a goldsmith before being taken to the coast, where he was put on a slave ship. Here he describes what it was like on board:

"This wretched situation was again aggravated by … the chains … and the filth of the [toilets] into which the children often fell, and were almost suffocated. The shrieks of the women, and the groans of the dying, rendered [made] the whole a scene of horror."

▲ *The opening pages of* The Interesting Narrative of Olaudah Equiano *or* Gustavus Vassa, the African.

Arriving in Barbados

The journey across the Atlantic took many weeks, during which time Equiano was whipped for not eating and had thought about jumping overboard to drown himself. Here he describes arriving in the Caribbean:

"At last we came in sight of the island of Barbadoes, at which the whites on board gave a great shout, and made many signs of joy to us … Many merchants and planters now came on board … and examined us attentively. They also made us jump, and pointed to the land, signifying we were to go there. We thought by this we should be eaten by these ugly men … [but they] told us we were not to be eaten, but to work."

The slave auctions

After being taken off the ship, Equiano and the other enslaved Africans were to be sold to the highest bidder:

"On a signal given [at the beat of a drum], the buyers rush at once into the yard where the slaves are confined, and make choice of [who] they like best. The noise … terrified Africans … there were several brothers, who, in the sale, were sold in different lots; and it was very moving on this occasion to see and hear their cries at parting… Why are parents to lose their children, brothers their sisters, or husbands their wives?"

▼ This 18th-century wood carving shows enslaved Africans being taken to a slave ship.

Being sold

Equiano wasn't sold at the slave auction. Instead, he ended up working in the fields in Virginia State, USA, weeding grass and picking stones from the ground until he was noticed:

"This gentleman, whose name was Michael Henry Pascal, was a lieutenant in the Royal Navy … While he was at my master's house it happened that he saw me, and liked me so well that he made a purchase of me. I think I have often heard him say he gave thirty or forty pounds sterling for me."

Equiano's experience was different from many enslaved Africans, as he did not work on plantations or in the houses of the slave owners. However, he did witness the brutality of the slave trade, which he recorded in his book.

Arriving in the Americas

When the slave ships arrived in the Americas, the owners had to make sure that their 'goods' – the enslaved Africans – were ready to be sold. In order to make sure that they received the best price for their slaves, the owners washed the Africans in palm oil to make their skin look healthy and the men were shaved as well. There were a variety of ways in which the slaves were sold; the auction, 'the scramble' or even door-to-door.

▲ *This illustration is of a slave auction taking place in the Americas in 1861.*

The auction

These are extracts from the work of Mary Prince (see pages 34–35), who was one of the few women to record their experiences as a slave when she wrote her autobiography in 1831.

"The auctioneer, who was to offer us for sale like sheep or cattle, arrived, and asked my mother which was the eldest. She said nothing but pointed to me. He took me by the hand, and led me out into the middle of the street and, turning me slowly round showed me to everyone at the auction. I was soon surrounded by strange men, who examined and handled me in the same manner that a butcher would a calf or a lamb he was about to buy ... I was then put up for sale. The bidding commenced at a few pounds and gradually rose to fifty-seven ... the people who stood by said that I had fetched a great sum for so young a slave."

The scramble

Alexander Falconbridge saw a slave scramble, where buyers rushed to purchase 250 enslaved Africans:

"On a day appointed, the Negroes were landed and placed together in a large yard belonging to the merchants to whom the ship was consigned. As soon as the hour agreed on arrived, the doors of the yard were suddenly thrown open and in rushed a considerable number of purchasers, with all the ferocity of brutes. Some instantly seized such of the Negroes as they could conveniently lay hold of with their hands. Others being prepared with several handkerchiefs tied together, circled as many as they were able ... The poor astonished Negroes were so terrified by these proceedings, that several of them, through fear, climbed over the walls of the courtyard and ran wild about the town, but were soon hunted down and retaken."

The slaves who were not sold at auction or by scramble were known as 'refuse slaves' and some ended up being sold in pubs to anyone who would take them. This could be for as little as £1.

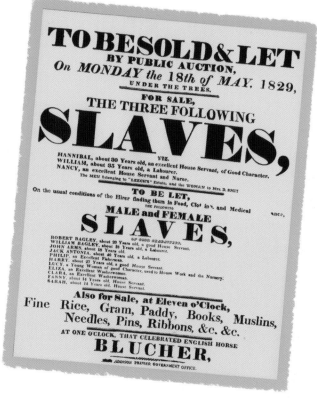

▲ A poster advertising slaves for sale and to let at a public auction.

▲ A US slave street sale in 1860. Slavery had been abolished in most places by this time.

Sugar!

Can you guess what everyday item, which you may sprinkle over your cereal, was known as 'white gold'? Today, it is hard for us to believe, but 300 years ago sugar was such an important foodstuff that it gave birth to an entire industry, worth millions of pounds. However, you might also want to think about this disturbing fact. Most of this money resulted from the back-breaking work of enslaved Africans, who were used in their thousands on the sugar plantations in Brazil and the Caribbean.

Growing sugar

There are a number of different stages before sugar cane, which looks like tall plants of bamboo, can be turned into granular sugar. One of the first jobs the slaves had to do was to plant the new crops of sugar cane. To fill half a hectare of land would need between 5,000 and 8,000

▲ *A painting called* Slaves Cutting The Sugar Cane *painted in Antigua, 1823 by William Clark.*

plants. This was a very slow and painful job, as the lines of slaves had to walk across the fields bending down to drop the seeds – by hand – into the ground. Once the crop was ready to be harvested, which took between 9 and 24 months depending on the climate, the cane had to be cut down. This was another tough job. The canes had to be cut close to the ground to get the maximum amount of sugary cane juice.

Refining the sugar

The next stage was to take the sugar canes to the mills to crush them between giant rollers. This was very dangerous and many slaves got terrible injuries after becoming caught in the machines. The rollers worked 24 hours a day, so the slaves had to work in different shifts. Once the cane juice was collected, it had to be boiled in huge vats. This was another very dangerous job, and there were many slaves who were burned very badly as they had no protection against the boiling liquid. This process eventually turned the liquid into sugar crystals, which then had to be broken up with pickaxes and shovels. Finally, the crystal sugar was put into barrels known as 'hogsheads' and any remaining liquid – called molasses – was allowed to drip out. By the 1850s, each year every slave working on sugar plantations was expected to produce five hogsheads of sugar and 1,140 litres of molasses.

▲ In this engraving from 1596, you can see the rollers and hogheads used at the mills.

What was it like to work on the plantations?

As well as working on the sugar plantations, there were many other jobs that slaves did in the Caribbean and the southern states of the USA. Outside, field slaves tended labour intensive crops, including tobacco, cotton and rice. Inside, house slaves had many daily tasks.

Field slaves

The 'field slaves' worked outside, spending 12 hours a day weeding, pulling up stones, spreading manure, planting crops, cutting wood and looking after the animals. Working in the rice fields was particularly unhealthy, as the slaves worked for weeks on end in the muddy water under the

▲ Both field slaves and house slaves received terrible punishments, including public whippings like the one shown here.

punishing heat of the Sun. The overseer made sure that all the slaves worked under the constant threat of physical punishment.

House slaves

There were also slaves working in the houses of the plantation owners, known as 'house slaves'. They had to cook, clean, serve meals and look after the children. Although it seemed like their jobs were easier than those of the field slaves, the house slaves often found themselves being watched very closely and could be punished for the smallest mistake.

Punishments

One of the ways in which the slaves were controlled was through the punishments that were handed out on a daily basis. The most common was the use of the whip, and slaves often received between 10 and 100 lashes of the whip for the smallest error. William Wells Brown (1816–84) was a young boy working as a house slave when he heard his mother being punished:

"Though the field was some distance from the house, I could hear every crack of the whip, and every groan and cry of my poor mother … After giving her ten lashes, the sound of the whip ceased, and I returned to my bed, and found no consolation but in my tears."

Other punishments included being forced to wear an iron ring around their neck, which made it impossible to sleep lying down, or being forced to wear an iron muzzle which made it impossible to talk.

If slaves tried to escape they could be branded with hot irons, or tied up and hung over an open fire. Some were beaten so severely that they died as a result of their injuries.

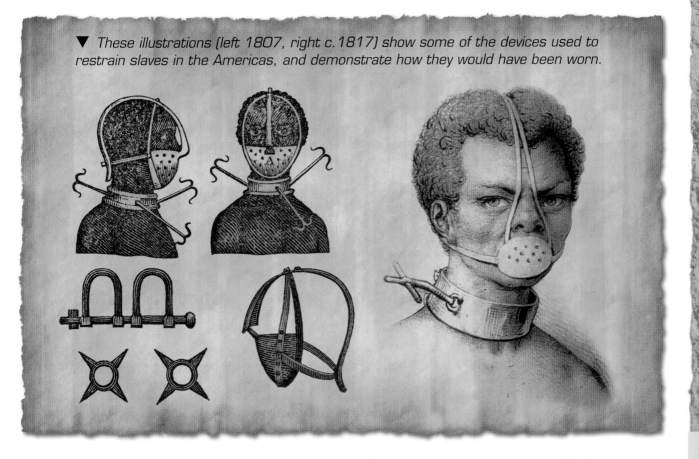

▼ These illustrations (left 1807, right c.1817) show some of the devices used to restrain slaves in the Americas, and demonstrate how they would have been worn.

What was it like to live on the plantations?

The living conditions on the plantations were difficult. The huts that the slaves lived in were similar to those provided for the animals. During the summer they were baking hot; in the winter they were freezing cold. The slaves were only given limited clothing by their owners, so often had to make their own or barter (exchange) at Sunday markets.

▲ *A group of slaves outside their hut in Georgia State, USA, in the mid-19th century.*

Julius Lester (b.1939) wrote in his children's book *To Be A Slave*:

"My pillow was a stick of wood. The bedding was a rough blanket … The cabin is constructed of logs without floor or window … In stormy weather rain pours in. Our dress was made of cheap cloth; for the children nothing but a shirt; for the older ones a pair of trousers or a gown … Besides these in the winter, a round jacket or overcoat, a wool hat once in two or three years … and a pair of coarse shoes once a year."

Family life

It was almost impossible for the enslaved Africans to experience anything resembling that we consider a 'normal' family life. As soon as they arrived in the Americas, families were separated, with children often being sold separately from their parents. However, slaves were encouraged by their owners to get married – but not because they felt sorry for them. The owners wanted children to be born so that there would be future generations of slaves, and there was also a belief that male slaves were less likely to run away or cause any problems if they were married. Some slave owners raped their female slaves and consequently there were many mixed-race children born. These were known as mulattoes.

Illness

Many slaves became ill as a result of the physically demanding work, the poor living conditions and the difficult environment on the plantations. The slave owners were often concerned that the slaves were pretending to be ill to avoid work, and punished them if they did not believe them. It was often the wife of the plantation owner who treated any slave that was ill. This happened because the slave owners were worried that if the slaves got access to medicines, they could use them to poison their masters. Amongst the slaves, women were usually the ones who would treat the ill, often using herbal remedies that had been brought with them from Africa.

▲ *Enslaved Africans in South Carolina, USA, 1863, with four children of their European owners. Two years later, slavery was abolished in the USA.*

Mary Prince

Mary Prince was born in Bermuda in 1788, and because both of her parents were slaves, she was born into slavery. At the age of 12 she was sold for the first time and separated from her family, whom she never saw again.

Mary had a series of brutal owners who regularly whipped her. For many years she had to work on the salt farms on Turks Island. This was a particularly hard job, and Mary may have lost her eyesight as a result of the harsh conditions. When she was sold to another owner in Antigua, Mary met a freeman called Daniel James and they got married in 1826. However, Mary moved to England with her owners in 1828, and as slavery had been abolished in England in 1807, she was able to run away and get her freedom. (The slave trade continued in the USA until 1865, and until 1888 in South America.) Mary wanted to return to Antigua to be with her husband, but she was told that if she went back she would have to go back into slavery. Instead, she stayed in London and worked with members of the slavery abolitionist movement. Mary became the first woman to record her experiences as a slave when she published her autobiography, *The History of Mary Prince, A West Indian Slave* in 1831.

Here are a few extracts from Mary's book describing her experiences as a slave in the West Indies:

▲ *No photographs of Mary exist, but many families such as this had slave girls to care for a young child.*

Punished

Mary was working for a new mistress who was particularly cruel to her:

"My mistress set about instructing me in my tasks. She taught me to do all sorts of household work; to wash and bake, pick cotton and wool, and wash floors, and cook. And she taught me (how can I ever forget it!) more things than these; she caused me to know the exact difference between the smart of the rope, the cart-whip, and the cow-skin, when applied to my naked body by her own cruel hand."

Turks Island

When Mary was sold to a new owner in Turks Island, she had to work on the salt farms. This was extremely demanding work in the heat of the Sun and involved standing in water for hours on end:

▲ *Workers producing salt on Turks Island today, still part of British Overseas Territory.*

"I was given a half barrel and a shovel, and had to stand up to my knees in the water, from four o'clock in the morning till nine … and worked through the heat of the day; the Sun flaming upon our heads like fire, and raising salt blisters in those parts which were not completely covered. Our feet and legs, from standing in the salt water for so many hours, soon became full of dreadful boils."

Fighting back

Here, Mary describes fighting back against her terrible treatment. This was a brave thing to do as many slaves were killed by their owners for daring to resist:

"One time I had plates and knives in my hand, and I dropped both plates and knives, and some of the plates were broken. He struck me so severely for this, that at last I defended myself, for I thought it was high time to do so. I then told him I would not live longer with him, for he was a very indecent man – very spiteful, and too indecent; with no shame for his servants, no shame for his own flesh. So I went away to a neighbouring house and sat down and cried till the next morning, when I went home again, not knowing what else to do."

▲ *A meeting of the Anti-Slavery Society, which Mary became part of while she was in Britain.*

How did enslaved Africans maintain their culture?

Despite the working and living conditions that enslaved Africans had to put up with, they were still able to create strong communities which allowed them to keep their ties with their roots in Africa.

▲ *This painting from the 1830s shows enslaved Africans dancing and playing music.*

Shared bonds

Plantation owners separated slaves from others who came from the same parts of Africa, creating a class system which divided the slaves based on their different jobs. But despite this and the situation they found themselves in, slave communities were able to use religion, music and language to bond together.

Music

One of the strongest connections with Africa came from the music that the slaves brought with them to the Americas. There were many instruments, including pipes and drums, that were very important ways of sharing the African culture and passing on their history through the generations. Slaves were encouraged to sing by many plantation owners, as they realised it was an effective way to work. However, some plantation owners did not allow drums to be played. They were worried that the drums could be used as a signal to other slaves to rise up against them. At the weekends, especially on Saturday evenings and on Sundays, enslaved Africans came together to sing and dance, and try to forget the horrors of their daily lives.

Religion

There were many different religions in Africa, with local traditions mixing with Islam and Christianity. However, most enslaved Africans in the Americas were baptised into the Christian Church. This was one of the ways in which Africans were forced into losing their identity (another was that they were given new names by their owners). Some slaves took refuge in the teachings of the Bible; that they would be rewarded for their difficult life when they got to heaven. Others adapted the Christian teachings so they fitted closer to the traditional African ideas. There were also African cults, such as Voodoo and Obeah, which developed in the West Indies and are still practised today.

Language

The enslaved Africans came from many different countries in Africa, so there was no single language spoken by them. As a result, a new language evolved which combined some of the African languages with English or French. This was known as Creole. The plantation owners often talked to the slaves in Creole.

▼ *The slaves of a white family in South Carolina, USA, gather to worship on a Sunday in 1863.*

What was the legacy of slavery for Africa?

The effects of the Transatlantic Slave Trade can still be felt today, over 200 years after the final abolition of slavery in 1888.

Rich and poor

Many historians have argued that the main consequence of slavery was that the countries which benefited from the work Africans did on the plantations, such as Britain and the USA, continue to remain among the richest countries in the world. Those countries that slaves were taken from in Africa remain some of the poorest. West Africa, in particular, lost millions of its people who took with them the skills and talents, which could have been used to develop their own countries.

Racism and fair trade

The other legacy of slavery is racism. It is impossible to deny how damaging the idea that Black Africans were inferior to white Europeans has been throughout modern society. Despite attempts to promote fair trade between countries, laws to promote equality between races and the success of individuals, such as US President Barack Obama, in reaching the highest positions in society, there is still a long way to go before there is genuine equality.

▲ A shop in Ajegunle slum, Lagos, Nigeria. The slum is home to 5 million people living in poverty.

War and slavery

It is difficult to place a precise figure on how many Africans were enslaved and transported to the Americas during the whole of the Transatlantic Slave Trade. Estimates range from 10 to 15 million men, women and children, with the majority being aged between 15 and 25. The impact that this had on West Africa was devastating. There were many wars

▲ *Wars continued in Africa until around 1900, with Arab traders enslaving Africans. Here a trader is cutting a dying slave from his yoke.*

that broke out in order to get slaves to be sold, with weapons supplied by the European traders. The explorer John Speke who travelled throughout Africa in the 1860s said: *"To catch slaves is the first thought of every chief in the interior [of Africa], hence fights and slavery impoverish the land"* and he wrote this 30 years after the slave trade had been abolished!

Colonialism

One of the most significant lasting impacts of the Transatlantic Slave Trade was the eventual control of Africa by European countries. In 1884, at the Conference of Berlin, the leaders of Britain, France, Germany, Italy and Belgium came together to decide which

parts of Africa they wanted to control. They actually used a ruler to draw lines on the map of Africa to show where the new borders would be – have a look at the borders of Egypt as the best example. The racism that had led to the enslavement of millions of Africans also led to the idea that they should be ruled over by Europeans. It wasn't until the 1960s that most African countries reclaimed their independence. Today, African countries are still fighting the legacy of war, debt and inequality left by the Transatlantic Slave Trade.

▲ *The run-down dockside seen from Elmina Castle. Money is needed to fund development and preservation in many African countries.*

A timeline of the Transatlantic Slave Trade

c.300 The Kingdom of Ghana is founded

c.1200 The Kingdom of Mali is founded

1441 The first record of Africans being enslaved and taken to Portugal

1481 Elmina, a trading post which was used for holding enslaved Africans, is built by the Portuguese

1493 The Treaty of Tordesillas divides the New World between Portugal and Spain

1562 Sir John Hawkins becomes the first Englishman to trade in African slaves

1607 The British colony of Jamestown is set up on the east coast of America

1660 The Royal African Company set up by the British to trade slaves from Africa

1745 Olaudah Equiano born in Essaka in the kingdom of Benin (now Ghana)

1750 – 1800 The height of the Transatlantic Slave Trade – at least 3 million Africans are transported to the Americas

1781 The case of the slave ship Zong, 133 slaves were thrown overboard leading to a court case claiming for insurance

c1788 Mary Prince born in Bermuda

1789 Olaudah Equiano publishes his autobiography ' The Interesting Narrative'

1807 The abolition of the Slave Trade

1811 Slave trading by Britons becomes a crime punished by transportation to Australia for 14 years

1814 Treaty of Paris, which ended the Napoleonic Wars, included a clause against the slave trade

1821 Import of slaves to Cuba made illegal

1831 Import of slaves to Brazil made illegal

1833 The abolition of slavery in the British Empire

1839 Royal Navy ships are given the power to stop and search ships which are suspected of carrying slaves. If slaves were found they would be confiscated.

1873 Holding of slaves by British subjects in East Africa becomes a criminal offence

1874 Slave dealing abolished in the Gold Coast

1875 Slave children in the Gold Coast are freed

1901 Slavery abolished in Nigeria

1928 Slavery abolished in Sierra Leone

Websites and Bibliography

Websites

http://www.blackhistory4schools.com/slavetrade/
An excellent set of resources related to the Transatlantic Slave Trade

http://www.recoveredhistories.org/
A website dedicated to 18th and 19th century literature based on the Transatlantic Slave Trade

http://www.nationalarchives.gov.uk/pathways/blackhistory/africa_caribbean/africa_trade.htm
From the National Archives website

http://abolition.e2bn.org/slavery.html
A very useful website looking at the origins of the Transatlantic Slave Trade as well as the Middle Passage and life on the Plantations

http://www.history.com/topics/slavery
The history of slavery in America

http://www.digitalhistory.uh.edu/era.cfm?eraID=6&smtID=1
An interactive website based on the history of slavery

http://docsouth.unc.edu/neh/equiano1/equiano1.xml
Olaudah Equiano's autobiography 'An Interesting Narrative'

http://www.spartacus.schoolnet.co.uk/USAslavery.htm
A comprehensive guide to all aspects of the slave trade

Bibliography

Burton A, *Women's Slave Narratives*, Dover Publications Inc, 2006

Equiano O, *The Interesting Narrative of Olaudah Equiano or Gustavus Vassa the African*, Penguin, 1996

Foster N, *Out of Slavery*, Redcliffe Publishing, 2004

Hinds D, *Black Peoples of the Americas*, Collins Educational, 1992

Lester J, *To be a Slave*, Puffin Books, 1998

Louis Gates Jr. H [Ed], *The Classic Slave Narratives*, Signet Classic, 2002

Rees B and Sherwood M, *Black Peoples of the Americas*, Heinemann, 1992

Rees R, *Britain and the Slave Trade*, Heinemann, 1995

Sherwood K and Sherwood M, *Britain, The Slave Trade and Slavery from 1562 to the 1880s*, Savannah Press, 2007

Smith N, *Black Peoples of the Americas*, OUP, 1992

Tibbles A [Ed], *Transatlantic Slavery, Against Human Dignity*, Liverpool University Press, 1994

Walvin J, *Slavery to Freedom*, Pitkin Publishing, 2007

Glossary

Abolition To put an end to something completely.

Americas The word used to describe all the lands of both North and South America.

Bacterial pathogen A type of bacteria capable of causing disease.

Barracoon These were holding pens where enslaved Africans were kept before being loaded onto the slave ships.

Barter A form of trade where one person exchanges his goods for another's.

BCE (Before the Common Era) A system of numbering dates to show that the number refers to a date before the current era.

Branding Burning a mark into an object, animal or person with hot metal. Used by slave owners to mark ownership of their slaves.

CE (Common Era) A system of numbering dates to show that they are from the current era.

Chattel slavery A form of slavery where Africans were seen as the property of their owners.

Christianity The religion based on the teachings of Jesus Christ.

Creole A language spoken by some enslaved Africans which was a mixture of African languages with European languages, such as English and French.

Culture The arts, beliefs and traditions of a particular society.

Domesday Book The records collected by the Norman rulers of England in the 11th century to show land ownership etc.

Explorer A person who travels to a foreign country to learn about it. European explorers are often described as 'discovering' a country, meaning they brought it to the attention of people back home.

Favourable winds For sailors, winds that will take their ship in the right direction.

Field slaves The enslaved Africans that worked in the fields growing and harvesting crops such as tobacco, sugar and cotton.

Freeman A person who is not a slave.

Guinea The name given to West Africa by the Portuguese.

House slaves The enslaved Africans that worked in the houses of the plantation owners doing cooking, cleaning and looking after children.

Indigo Deep blue plant dye for cloth.

Islam The religion based on the teachings of the Prophet Muhammad (*peace be upon him*).

Ivory The tusk of an elephant used to make objects such as piano keys, knife handles etc.

Middle East Term used to refer to countries stretching from Turkey to northern Africa and across to Iran and including Egypt, Israel, Iraq, Saudi Arabia, Libya and many others.

Middle Passage The part of the Transatlantic Slave Trade where enslaved Africans were taken from Africa to the Americas. The journey lasted between 6 and 8 weeks and many Africans died from the terrible conditions.

Molasses Thick, sugary syrup.

Mulatto The name given to a child born from a mixed race background, usually with a black African mother and a white European father.

Negroes Word used to describe Black people from Africa.

Persia The old name for the country of Iran.

Plantation Large farms that the enslaved Africans were forced to work on, growing crops such as sugar, tobacco and cotton.

Pyramid In ancient times, a huge monument built in pyramid shape to act as a tomb for a royal person.

Racism The theory that some races of people are more intelligent and superior to others.

Rape Forcing someone to have sex against their will.

Shackles A type of metal restraint used to tie slaves together or to a ship.

Slave auction An auction is a public sale. Enslaved Africans were sold at an auction to the highest bidder.

Slave scramble Buyers would rush around the enslaved Africans and grab as many as they could.

Slavery When someone is forced to work for another person and loses all of their freedoms and rights.

Transatlantic Slave Trade The name given to the enslavement and forced removal of millions of Africans from Africa to the Americas between the 16th and 19th centuries.

Triangular trade The journey of the slave ships which moved from Europe to Africa, to the Americas and back to Europe.

Tribe Group of people linked by family or other ties who share the same traditions and culture.

Vat Huge tub or other container for storing or heating liquids.

West Indies Large group of islands in the Caribbean Sea and including Barbados, Jamaica, Antigua and the Turks Islands.

Yoke A piece of wood shaped to fit a person's shoulders or to fit a working animal. Used in the slave trade to prevent slaves from running away as the yokes of each slave were joined together by chains.

Index

These are the lists of contents for the titles in *Black History*:

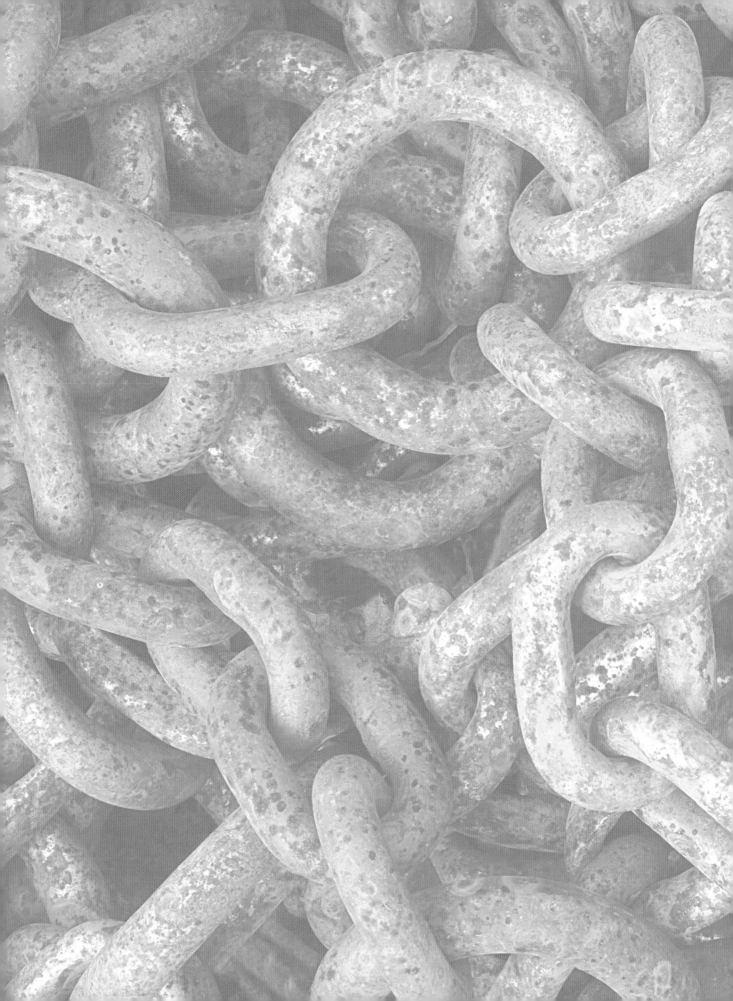

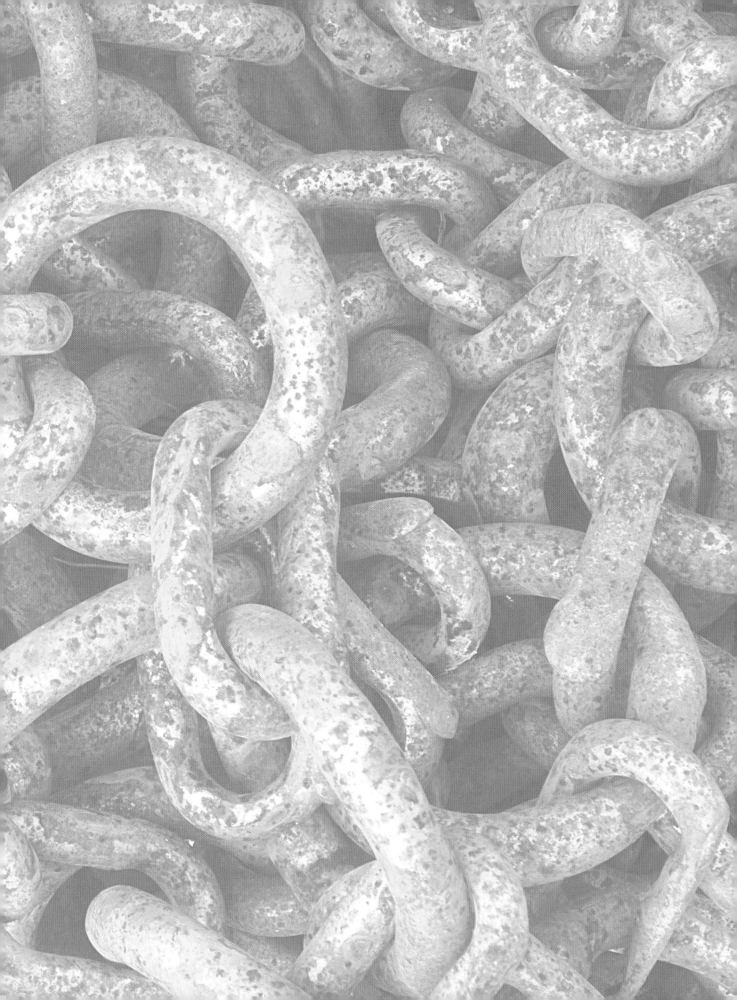

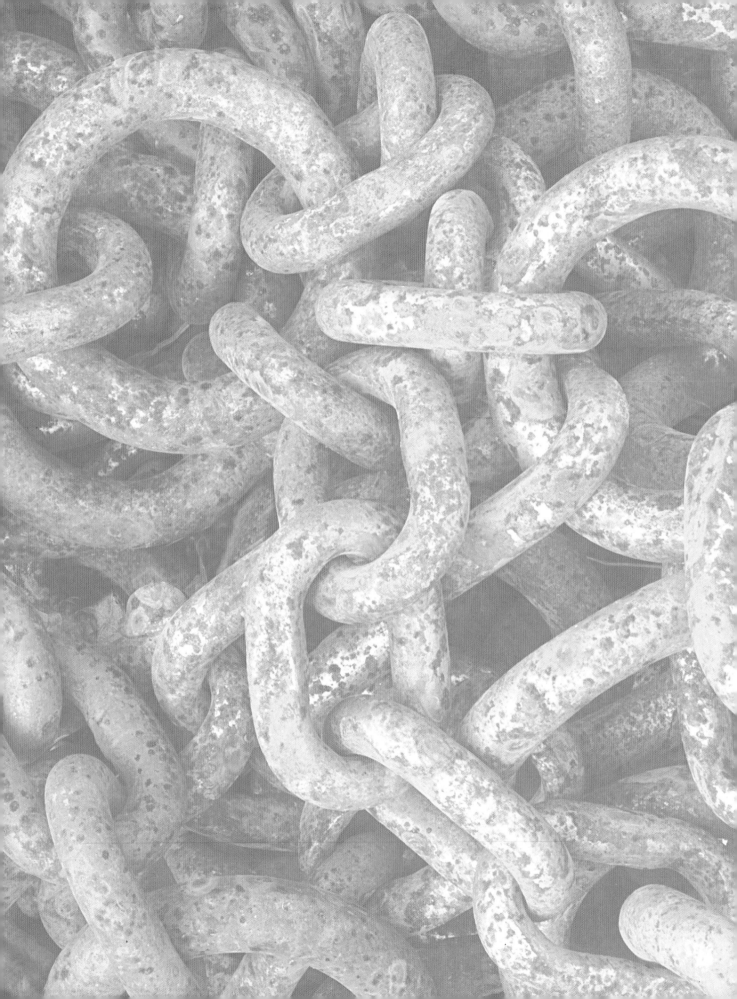